Easy Phonics Words

king

kitten

kilt

Illustrated by Fred Blunt

Reading consultants:
Alison Kelly and Anne Washtell
Roehampton University

Notes for parents

About phonics

Phonics is a way of teaching children to read by breaking words down into combinations of sounds or **phonemes**. There are 44 phonemes in the English language. Some are represented by single letters, like the c - a - t sounds in the word **cat**. Others are represented by more than one letter, like the sh - ar sounds in the word **shark**.

Listen to the phonemes

You can find a full list of phonemes, together with an online pronunciation guide, on the Very First Reading website, **www.usborne.com/ veryfirstreading*** – go to the Resources area and scroll down to **Pronouncing the phonemes**.

Using this book

In this book you will find words containing 43 of the 44 phonemes in their most common spellings (the 44th, the "zh" sound in words such as **vision**, is usually taught at a later stage). This is a great way to learn and remember new words, and ideal for reading and spelling practice. Choose a page and look for the featured phoneme in all the words on the page. Can you think of any more words with that same phoneme?

*US readers go to **www.veryfirstreading.com**

d

duck

dog

dish

dinner

doll

e

nest

well

net

leg

pen

hen

egg

shell

f ff

fan

cliff

fin fish

fork

coffee

fist

cuff

foot

h

hill

hut

hat

hood

hutch

hand

horn

j

jester

jam

jar

jacket

m

moon

man

milk

mug

mop

map

moth

n

nail

nut

nest

north

ng

wing

morning

swing

ping-pong

king

ring

oa

foal

cloak

foam

boat

toast

toad

or

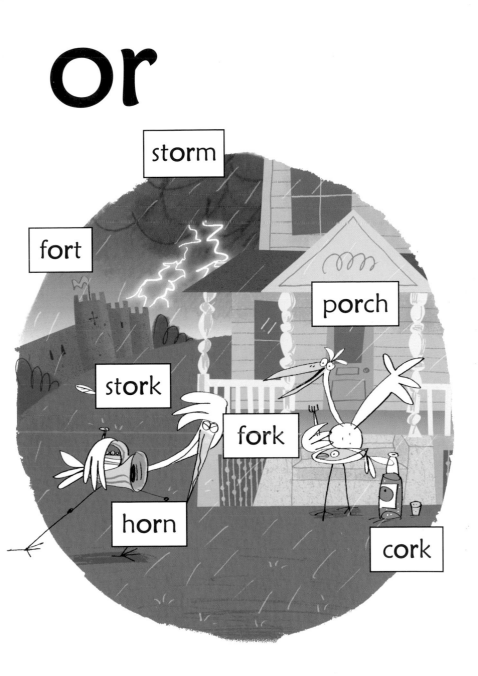

storm

fort

porch

stork

fork

horn

cork

ow

owl

town

clown

crowd

crowd

crown

cow

frown

p

park

pond

pets

picnic

painting

picnic

pig

paint

qu

quiz

queen

quilt

r

rain

road

rat

rabbit

radish

rug

reeds

river

sh

shed

sheep

fish

shark

shell

t

tennis

tent

towel

tail

ticket

th

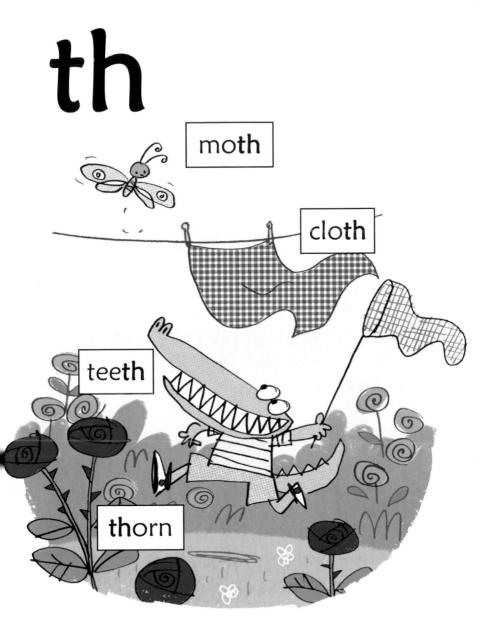

moth

cloth

teeth

thorn

u

sun

bus

hut

duck

mug

nut

plum

butter

slug

ur

church

curls

burger

surfer

burglar

turnip

ure

X

boxer

wax

box

fox

y

yak

yogurt

Edited by Mairi Mackinnon
Designed by Caroline Spatz

owl

clown

cow

First published in 2011 by Usborne Publishing Ltd., Usborne House,
83-85 Saffron Hill, London EC1N 8RT, England. www.usborne.com
Copyright © 2011 Usborne Publishing Ltd.

USBORNE VERY FIRST READING

There are twenty-four more titles in the **Usborne Very First Reading** series, which has been specially developed to help children learn to read.

To find out more about the structure of the series, go to **www.usborne.com/veryfirstreading**